Can I Be a Christian
Christian
WITHOUT BEING
Weird?

Can I Be a Christian
WITHOUT BEING
Weird?

·······························

KEVIN
JOHNSON

BETHANY HOUSE PUBLISHERS
MINNEAPOLIS, MINNESOTA 55438

Published by Bethany House Publishers
A Ministry of Bethany Fellowship, Inc.
6820 Auto Club Road, Minneapolis, Minnesota 55438

Printed in the United States of America

Library of Congress Cataloging-in-Publication Data

Johnson, Kevin.
    Can I be a Christian without being weird? / Kevin Johnson
       p. cm.
    Summary: A collection of devotional readings and suggested Bible passages addressing prayer, self-esteem, knowing God, and what it means to be a disciple.

    1. Teenagers—Prayer-books and devotions—English.
[1. Prayer books and devotions. 2. Christain life.]
I. Title.
BV4850.J64   1992
242'.63—dc20   92-15804
                                                 CIP
ISBN 1–55661–281–8   AC

To

Lyn, Nathaniel, and Karin,

As together we seek first God and His Kingdom

Kevin Johnson is an associate pastor at Elmbrook Church in metro Milwaukee, where he works with almost 400 sixth–ninth graders. While his training includes an M.Div. from Fuller Theological Seminary and a B.A. in English and Print Journalism from the University of Wisconsin-River Falls, his current interests run along the lines of cycling, in-line skating, books, guitar, and shortwave radio. Kevin and his wife, Lyn, live in Wisconsin with their two children, Nathaniel and Karin.

Contents

Part 3: Putting a Lid on Peer Fear

Part 4: Digging for the Good Stuff

PART 1

Busting
Down the
WALLS

1

What Happens When the Marshmallows Are Gone?

The campfire flared, lighting up a dozen sweaty teenage faces.

"So what *are* you into? What makes you happy?" I asked Vicki. I hadn't been able to figure her out yet, and my attempts to be her friend over the past few days hadn't worked. From what I had seen, nothing seemed to thrill her.

"Money makes me happy," Vicki said. "I want to be rich."

"How come?"

"I like to go to the mall." She gave me a look that meant *Isn't that obvious, you stupid pastor?* Once I thought about it, she did look as though she knew her malls.

"What do you do when the malls close?" I continued.

"Not much." Silence.

"And that's fun?" someone asked.

Vicki could tell we weren't impressed.

"Marshmallows!" she said suddenly. "I like marshmallows." She held up a marshmallow, one she was oozing between her fingers, to demonstrate her sincerity. "Marshmallows make me happy."

My last question to her fell unanswered as she looked away, into the fire. "So what happens when the marshmallows are gone?"

Marshmallows. Aren't they what being your age is all about? All of life's thrills and peak moments: an afternoon kicking around with friends, a whoosh down a water slide, a new tape in your Walkman, winning at sports, your dog jumping at the door for you after school—they're marshmallows. Sweet. Fast, yet savory. Sugar-roasted hot on a stick. Lick your lips to get it all.

But is that *all* there is? If you admit there might be more to life than marshmallows, peers who plan to coast carefree through teenhood might think you're weird. Too serious. Too much on the fringe. They might leave you sitting alone at the campfire, humming a tune to yourself that no one else knows. It's hard enough hiding stuff people might laugh at—looks, clumsiness, a less-than-designer wardrobe, brains or lack of them—without handing out something else to be rejected.

Vicki, however, ignored some important questions: What do you do when the marshmallows are gone? What do you do when the bag is empty—when your Walkman starts eating tapes, your Gameboy batteries die, or friends move away? How do you feel when you're alone and quiet long enough to wonder, *Why am I here? Why am I the way I am? Does anybody care about me?*

Or how about these: Where do you turn when your parents fight? When you have a tough time at school? When even your friends talk behind your back? Where do you run when it seems no one understands you— when your parents say they're "disappointed" with you, and your teachers say "you aren't living up to your potential"?

Maybe you want to figure things out, and have a hunch that God has something to do with the answers. Even so, you don't want a faith that makes you strange: "Hi. I'm a Christian. Just call me Zork, because I act like I'm from another planet."

Is it possible to follow Christ without being weird?

Don't worry, it has been done. Being a Christian

won't make you weird. (At least not any stranger than you already might be.) And remember, there *is* life beyond marshmallows—things like being friends with God, taking a stand without being strange, surviving peer fear to live God's best for you. Being a Christian may bring excitement different from what a lot of your peers expect, but I guarantee it's a riot that outlasts a gazillion bags of marshmallows.

You may want to know more about God but are having a hard time understanding the Bible. This book will make it easier for you to dig in and find something helpful.

Read a chapter at a time. I promise, this one is the longest in the book. You'll need a Bible to look up and read the passages where it says ☑ **Read.** (That gets you out of this book and into the Bible—the real stuff.) To dig deeper, you can do the same with the other verses (listed in parentheses) that pop up here and there. At the end of each reading are some verses that pick out highlights of the passage. You might find something you want to memorize.

So grab a Bible—get one that's easy to read—and find someplace quiet. Bring a snack if you want. (And don't forget the marshmallows.)

2
Lost and Alone

Tree branches whipped Sue's face and scratched her arms and legs. She had been running on a logging trail in a thick forest when she realized the path no longer looked familiar. Scared, she ran faster but recognized even less. Her high from running quickly faded into confusion and fright. She turned and began running the other direction, but was soon lost even deeper in the darkening forest. Hours later she crumpled from exhaustion at the shore of a lake.

Have you ever been lost? What do you do?

Some people panic—like Sue. Other people refuse to admit they're lost. Most family vacations share one thing: dad or mom driving farther and farther down the wrong road to avoid the total embarrassment of stopping to ask directions. (Snickering from the backseat doesn't help!)

But some lost people stay calm and get directions. They backtrack in the woods and find a sign, or they pull into a gas station. They admit they need help figuring out exactly where they are and how to get where they want to go.

▶ **Read 2 Timothy 3:14–17. How does the Bible help Christians?**

If you want to get un-lost in the woods or on a road, you've got to stop to get directions. Because some hikers found Sue and led her out of the forest, she didn't die. Because drivers gulp down their pride and ask directions, a lot of family vacations are rescued. If you want to get un-lost in life, the passage you read says the Bible is the place to look. It teaches you to know God and helps you mature. It shows you the way to real life.

On the other hand, getting directions doesn't work if the directions you get aren't clear. But the Bible is "breathed by God" so that it provides perfect directions from the perfect God. If you look to God's Word, the Bible, for directions, you can trust what it says. It's your unique guidebook written by the ultimate guide, God himself.

You have known the holy Scriptures, which are able to make you wise for salvation through faith in Christ Jesus. All Scripture is God-breathed and is useful for teaching, rebuking, correcting and training in righteousness.

2 TIMOTHY 3:15–16

3

Hunger Pains

"My Sunday school class decided to read the Bible from cover to cover this year," Scott said. "I made it to January twenty-third—all the way through Leviticus and halfway into Numbers before I got swamped. That's three and a half books. But I still think I should do better."

Getting to know God isn't meant to be such a pain.

☑ **Read John 6:28–35. What do you think drew people to Jesus?**

No one has to force you to eat. You eat because you're hungry. Your stomach growls and you put something into it. Believe it or not, you get hunger pains for God. That's what draws you to Him. Your questions, problems, doubts, triumphs, failures, your dreams about things you want to be or do, the things you love and hate—those are hunger pains poking you to get nearer to God by spending time with Him and His Word.

But slow down—when you go out to eat you never say, "Give me one of everything, please," then try to eat it all. You find out what's best and start there. So why try to gulp the Bible down all at once? This book will help you start with a few of the Bible's choicest morsels, and later you can eat your way through the rest of the menu.

Even your loudest hunger pains quiet down if you think only about the vitamins, amino acids, and complex carbohydrates you get when you eat. What a way to wreck a meal! Who wants a plateful of *that*? You might as well have a nurse jab an intravenous needle into your arm to feed you. In the same way, if you always tell yourself, "This is good for me" or "I'm doing this because I have to" or "I have to finish the Bible by next month, or else," you'll lose your appetite for God. Reading your Bible for those reasons turns it cold and tasteless. It's like shoving yourself toward a meal you hate.

Food that you know tastes good will lure you closer. Jesus promises that He's that kind of food—food that satisfies better than anything else. *He* is what makes Bible reading something you do because you want to, not because you have to.

Then Jesus declared, "I am the bread of life. He who comes to me will never go hungry, and he who believes in me will never be thirsty."

JOHN 6:35

4

Why Would Anyone Want to See Jesus So Badly?

The man's spotless business suit became rumpled and grimy as he yanked himself into the tree. His pants caught on a sharp twig and ripped. After grunting loudly and sweating through his suit coat, he settled on a branch that bowed under his weight. People on the ground burst out laughing as they recognized the man.

The people? Your friends. The man? Your dad, trying to get a better shot with his camcorder at your first soccer game of the season.

Why would your dad—or your mom, or whoever—do that? Because he wants to see you and to show you off to whoever else will sit through the video.

☑ **Read Luke 19:1–10. Why would anyone want to see Jesus so badly?**

Zacchaeus (Zack-KEY-us) climbed a tree to see Jesus because he had heard that Jesus loved the unlovable—and Zacchaeus knew he wasn't exactly adored by the masses. As a corrupt tax collector, Zacchaeus cheated his countrymen and aided the occupying enemy, the Romans. He was pure slime, the worst of his society.

19

But Jesus picked Zacchaeus to share dinner with Him. Why?

Jesus walked right by the people who stood on the ground laughing at Zacchaeus, people who thought they were better than the awful tax collector, good enough to deserve Jesus' friendship. Zacchaeus had a need and showed it by climbing the tree. The others laughed at his honesty.

Zacchaeus did something strange because he knew he needed Jesus so badly. No one else did, even though every person in the crowd also needed Jesus as forgiver, master, and friend. Everyone should have been up in that tree.

You are special to God. He knew you before you were born. He sent His Son, Jesus, to live and die and rise again for you. And He comes now. "Listen!" He says. "I stand at the door and knock. If anyone hears my voice and opens the door, I will come in and eat [fellowship] with him, and he with me" (Revelation 3:20).

Are you "up in a tree"? Do you want to be? The starting point is to be like Zacchaeus. Admit that you need Jesus . . . and don't worry about who sees you.

He [Zacchaeus] wanted to see who Jesus was, but being a short man he could not, because of the crowd. So he ran ahead and climbed a sycamore-fig tree to see him, since Jesus was coming that way. When Jesus reached the spot, he looked up and said to him, "Zacchaeus, come down immediately. I must stay at your house today." So he came down at once and welcomed him gladly.

LUKE 19:3–6

5
The Wall

For almost thirty years, eastern Germany was walled off from western Germany, city from city, family from family, friend from friend. East Germans suffered through pollution, poverty, and brutal control of politics and religion, only dreaming of the freedoms enjoyed in the West, outside the wall. Anyone who tried to escape faced razor wire, dogs, land mines, and machine guns.

You probably wouldn't choose to live inside a wall in a country that's like a prison cell, separated from everything you enjoy. Yet you and I and every person who has ever lived are expert wall-builders who choose to separate ourselves from God and His goodness.

☛ Read Luke 15:11–20, 23–24. How does the son distance himself from his father?

We're all a lot like the son in the story (Romans 3:23). Wanting to grow up, we battle to do things our way—and we would act more like the son than we do if we thought we could get away with it.

Each time we disobey—when we sin by what we think, say or do—we lay a brick between ourselves and God. He doesn't build the wall; *we* do, each time we choose to sin. Sin separates us from God as we build that wall brick by brick. Sin makes it impossible for us to be God's friends.

Separation is also God's final punishment for wrongdoing. If we refuse God's way of demolishing the wall, we will discover that when we die, the wall cements for eternity (Romans 6:23). We'll find ourselves cut off from God and *everything* good He has made. No phone, TV, radio, or satellite dish will tie us to family or friends or God on the other side of the wall. Being cemented inside the wall—in hell—isn't a fairy tale off a heavy metal album cover. It's real.

Yet if you read further in Luke 15, you'll find that the son in the story came home to his waiting father. Our Father in heaven is waiting for us, too, so that *we* can be friends again with Him. To make this possible, God sent His son, Jesus Christ, to tear down the wall we have built. You just need to ask.

But while he was still a long way off, his father saw him and was filled with compassion for him; he ran to his son, threw his arms around him and kissed him. . . . "Let's have a feast and celebrate. For this son of mine was dead and is alive again."

LUKE 15:20, 23–24

6
Demolishing the Wall

Imagine the Beaver (the kid on the old TV show, not the animal) playing ball in the living room while his parents are gone. *Whizzz* flies the ball right through a beautiful vase. Eddie, Beaver's brother's friend, helps Beaver glue the vase back together and rearrange the flowers. Exit Eddie.

Enter Ward and June, Beaver's parents. June refills the vase with water. Uh-oh—it leaks. Ward brilliantly concludes that someone has broken the vase. Wally, Beaver's older brother, feels sorry for Beaver and takes the blame, telling his mother and father that he, not Beaver, broke the vase. Wally is grounded and misses his date with Mary Ellen.

That happens only in the make-believe world of black and white reruns, doesn't it? No one takes the punishment like that, does he?

Someone did.

☑ **Read Isaiah 53:4–12, especially 4–6. These Old Testament verses predict that Jesus will take the punishment others deserve. Whose blame does He take?**

Even though Jesus had never sinned and deserved no punishment, He chose to suffer for *our* sin: "He was pierced for our transgressions, he was crushed for our iniquities." Jesus was perfect, yet He suffered God's punishment for sin—death—so we wouldn't have to. He did what Wally did a billion times better.

Jesus died for everyone, but God requires each of us to accept that fact personally. Beaver needed to tell the truth about the vase, and we need to take responsibility for our sin. You can do that by praying, "God, I've sinned. I've broken your rules and disappointed you. God, I know that Jesus died in my place." That's the beginning of being a Christian. That's what Christians call "accepting Jesus as Savior and Lord."

If you accept that Jesus suffered your punishment for you, you won't be apart from God now or ever: "When people sin, they earn what sin pays—death. But God gives us a free gift—life forever in Christ Jesus our Lord" (Romans 6:23, NCV). Forgiveness through Christ demolishes the wall of sin between you and God. Not a brick stands. Not a pebble is left—not even a speck of dust. It's all been washed away by Christ's blood.

But he was pierced for our transgressions, he was crushed for our iniquities; the punishment that brought us peace was upon him, and by his wounds we are healed. We all, like sheep, have gone astray, each of us has turned to his own way; and the Lord has laid on him the iniquity of us all.

ISAIAH 53:5–6

7

The Principal's Office

Consider, for a moment, your feelings upon receiving an invitation to your principal's office. As you skip happily down the hall, you anticipate congratulations for your outstanding scholarship and behavior. You look forward to engaging conversation with the person who provides your intellectual motivation. You think fondly of the teacher who recommended you for this time of warm sharing with your best of friends, your principal.

Not really. Unless your past has been sparkling clean, you don't feel that way. You go to the principal's office with anger flaring like drawn guns, certain that you're entering enemy territory.

Read Hebrews 10:19–22. How is getting close to God different from going to the principal's office?

Wouldn't you have a radical change of attitude about your visit if the principal were your good friend? (You may need a blimp full of imagination to grasp that one, but try.) Your principal, your new-found friend, knows you inside out and still likes you, so you can be yourself. You rely on your friend to teach you the smarts and give you courage to stay out of trouble. Your principal is an incredible teacher, counselor, enforcer, and friend rolled into one. Whatever the problem—homework, relationships, the school bully, loneliness—he helps you through. If the principal were our best friend, instead of getting *sent* to the principal, we would *go* to the principal.

This same radical change happens between us and God when the wall of sin and separation crumbles. We go to God's office—His presence—without fear because Jesus took our punishment on the cross and won us total friendship with God.

Before becoming a Christian, we rebel, hate rules, make excuses for sin, and fear death and hell—the ultimate detention. After accepting Jesus as Savior and Lord, we learn friendship, trust, forgiveness, and openness to correction. We look forward to eternity in heaven with God, our best friend.

Don't be afraid to go to God. His door is always open.

Since we have confidence to enter the Most Holy Place by the blood of Jesus . . . let us draw near to God with a sincere heart in full assurance of faith, having our hearts sprinkled to cleanse us from a guilty conscience.

HEBREWS 10:19–22

8
Eleven Against One

Holly didn't know what to say to Mrs. Peterson. "I have piano on Mondays, ballet on Tuesdays, community theater on Thursdays," she rattled off. "I baby-sit most Saturday nights, and I have gymnastics three days a week after school. And I get lots of homework, too."

"So you're saying you can't work on the yearbook just one night a week," Mrs. Peterson replied. "You know that means you probably won't be able to work on the yearbook in high school, don't you? They want experienced editors."

"I know," Holly said. Then she decided to tell Mrs. Peterson the real reason. "It's just that it's the only night of the week I can go to youth group."

Holly said no to a good activity so she could say yes to a better one—staying involved with her Christian friends.

Read Hebrews 10:23–25. The writer of Hebrews just explained to his readers their fantastic new friendship with God through Christ. How does he tell them to keep it fresh?

The key is to keep meeting together. Since so many influences try to rip down your faith, you need to reinforce and rebuild yourself and your Christian friends through encouragement—talking, praying, sharing the excitement of being a Christian. Missing church or youth group hurts both you and the Christians you could be helping.

When church conflicts with another activity, you might be able to reschedule one or the other. But when you can't, church shouldn't lose, even when that means disappointing advisors or friends, or missing future opportunities. Getting and giving encouragement is that important.

Only a fool would walk out on a football field to take on a whole team by himself. He would look up, see eleven mammoths charging to stomp his body, and run crying off the field. Why do you think you can stay in the game alone as a Christian—where the opponent intends to kill you? (1 Peter 5:8). You need your team or you won't survive.

Let us hold unswervingly to the hope we profess, for he who promised is faithful. And let us consider how we may spur one another on toward love and good deeds. Let us not give up meeting together, as some are in the habit of doing, but let us encourage one another.

HEBREWS 10:23–25A

9

Total Healing

Minutes after the collision, paramedics wheeled 14-year-old Alec into the emergency room, where a doctor washed the boy's wounds and sent him home. The doctor didn't sew up the still-bleeding cuts; he didn't set Alec's broken bones or treat his internal injuries. Alec was left brain damaged, bent, and twisted until death.

Were that to happen to anyone we know, we would scream with fury and sue for millions. Why, then, do we get upset when God, the great doctor who wants to heal us totally, starts to go beyond washing our sins to treat the root of our problems? We like having our sins forgiven and knowing that we'll go to heaven, but we get angry when God wants to do surgery on our sin.

If sin is awful enough for Jesus to have to die for it, then it's awful enough for us to want to get rid of it.

God saves us not just from the punishment for sin, but from the power of sin to rule and wreck us.

☑ **Read 2 Corinthians 5:14–15. Why did Jesus die?**

Forgiveness is only the first part of God's cure for sin. Getting us to stop living for self and start following Christ is the second part. God won't let you have one without the other. Because Christ has died, our old sinful lives have died—and we have been born anew to live a better life.

There's nothing mysterious about how God works to change us. Once forgiven, we become friends with God. He uses that friendship to remake us. His Holy Spirit (Romans 8:1–17) lives in us, teaches us through the Bible, and empowers us beyond our natural abilities. That takes time, and sometimes it hurts, like surgery. But in the end, we're closer to becoming who God wants us to be.

God loves us too much to leave us twisting in pain, our sin and selfishness untreated.

———————

For Christ's love compels us, because we are convinced that one died for all, and therefore all died. And he died for all, that those who live should no longer live for themselves but for him who died for them and was raised again.

2 CORINTHIANS 5:14–15

10
Cow Pies

It's hard to think of anything more gross than playing Frisbee barefoot in a park and suddenly feeling something cold and wet ooze between your toes. You hop on one foot and shriek as you scramble to find a hose to clean off the dog or duck doo.

That's what the apostle Paul was thinking about when he wrote Philippians.

✍ Read Philippians 3:7–11. What does Paul think is the most important thing in life? What does he call everything else?

The things Paul once thought were important he calls "rubbish." The word he uses means "worthless trash" or "garbage" or, to be more vivid, "dung." Compared with knowing Christ, everything else is like stepping in a cow pie. That seems harsh, but it makes sense. Paul is saying that the *best* thing in life isn't what we have or what we do, but who we know: Christ.

That may sound a little too religious, like weirdness made for parents and pastors but not for you. What does it look like in real life?

It means wanting one thing more than anything else: to stick close to God, to do things the way God wants, whether that brings suffering or success. Being a believer is more than following rules, going to church or trying hard not to beat up your little brother. It's being best friends with the Lord of the universe.

Wait a minute, that doesn't mean quitting normal life and becoming a monk, but knowing, enjoying and serving God in everything you do.

Thinking you can actually be close to God isn't a cotton-candy dream that dissolves when wind and rain pelt it, when you try to make it work at home, in school or with friends. Paul's faith in God was tested by beatings, stonings, shipwrecks and persecutions, yet he (and lots of other believers) agree with the Bible when it says that it's better to live one short day close to God than a thousand without Him (Psalm 84:10).

———————

What is more, I consider everything a loss compared to the surpassing greatness of knowing Christ Jesus my Lord, for whose sake I have lost all things. I consider them rubbish, that I may gain Christ and be found in him.

PHILIPPIANS 3:8–9

11
Get Up and Go On

"I QUIT" Carlie screamed from halfway up the rock face. It was hard to tell from the ground whether her face was wet from tears or sweat, but she was shaking as she clung to the cliff. "I can't find anyplace to put my feet. I keep slipping! I can't do this anymore. Lower me down!"

Climbers don't always make it to the top. Not a lot of students pull straight *A*'s. Few musicians play in a recital and never miss a note. Being a Christian isn't any different—except that *no one* pulls it off perfectly. *No one* lives a flawless Christian life. If we think we live without sinning, we're fooling ourselves (1 John 1:8).

Paul admitted that. Just after he wrote in Philippians 3 that everything was a cow pie compared to knowing Christ, he told his readers he wasn't perfect. He sometimes missed his step.

📗 **Read Philippians 3:12–14. How did Paul cope with his mistakes?**

The worst thing about mistakes is that they make you want to quit. If you've botched a few assignments in a class at school, it's difficult to try to do better. You figure you're no good and that more effort won't change your grade anyway. There's no way to start over. Mess up a few classes or a semester and you start to think school isn't for you.

When you blow it as a Christian, you can't take back any hurt you've caused, and you still have to live with the consequences of messing up. Sin still offends God. But God makes a way to repair your relationship with Him and start over *right now*. A verse in 1 John tells how: "If we confess our sins, he is faithful and just and will forgive us our sins and purify us from all unrighteousness" (1:9).

That's part of what Paul meant by "forgetting what is behind." If you admit your sin to God, He forgives you and picks you up so you can press on toward the goal of knowing Christ completely. Don't ever give up on following Christ just because you fall down. There's no such thing as a Christian who never stumbles. Real Christians are the ones who get up and go on.

But one thing I do: Forgetting what is behind and straining toward what is ahead, I press on toward the goal to win the prize for which God has called me heavenward in Christ Jesus.

PHILIPPIANS 3:13–14

12

Look-alikes

Check this out in a crowd or at church: Can you spot couples who look alike—same hair, same clothes, same glasses, same expressions and gestures? Or do you see people who look like their pets—poodles, cats, horses, mice, frogs?

Before you mock them, think about yourself and your friends. Do you look like one another—same haircut, same clothes, same team jackets and shirts and hats, same earrings or watches? You probably walk the same and talk the same. Don't believe it? Try to see your group through the eyes of other ones at school. It's easy for you to pick out *other* cliques where, for better or for worse, members are clones of one another. Guess what? They think the same thing about your group.

When you spend time with someone, you gradually resemble each other in how you dress and act. The same thing happens spiritually. Who you hang around with shapes what your character looks like. When you spend time with Christ—talking with Him, reading His Word and being with His friends—you begin to look like Him.

☞ **Read Galatians 5:19–26. What qualities are rubbing off on you, thanks to the Holy Spirit, as you get to know God?**

The passage begins by telling what you would look like *without* God—full of rebellion, from sexual immorality to idolatry to drunkenness, jealousy and selfishness. Not that all non-Christians sport all those grotesque features—but since they hang out with God's enemies, that's what they look like more and more. If instead you choose to live close to Jesus, you begin to pick up all His good qualities, some of which are listed in verses 22 and 23.

People will see that you look more and more like Jesus as you know Him better (1 Corinthians 3:18). No one can fault you for being Jesus' look-alike ("against such things there is no law"). People can't criticize you for being loving, joyful, peaceful, patient, kind, good, faithful, gentle and self-controlled—and if they do, that just shows how messed up they are.

But the fruit of the Spirit is love, joy, peace, patience, kindness, goodness, faithfulness, gentleness and self-control.

GALATIANS 5:22–23

PART 2

Taking Out the TRASH

13
How Weird Do I Have to Be?

If you asked most teens to close their eyes and describe a Christian teenager, the picture wouldn't be pretty. *Bizarre looks*—hoisted pants, yuck hair, thick glasses, and a pocket protector or a funny little purse. *Strange talk*—they ask if you "know God," they always quote from the Bible, and they say "Praise Jesus" a lot. *Unbelievable actions*—they do stuff like running up to the lunchroom supervisor to explain who started the food fight and who threw what.

As a Christian you know you're supposed to be different. But how weird do you have to be?

Read Matthew 22:34–40. What does Jesus say are the two most important things you can do to show that you follow Him?

Jesus doesn't tell Christians to wear funny hats or to shave their heads. They don't necessarily hand out magazines at the mall or door-to-door. Their words don't always come out with "chapter 4, verse 12" attached. What makes a Christian different from other people is that he or she is (1) learning to love God totally ("love God with all your heart, soul and mind") and (2) learning to love others unselfishly ("love your neighbor as you love yourself").

Now in a way that *is* weird, because you won't find many people, kids or adults, following Jesus' command.

It's obvious that most people don't try hard to love God radically, though they claim they try to be good to others. Yet if you check out people's lives, most of the time—at school, home, with friends, at work—they gush selfishness. They consistently think of their own interests first. In that crowd, a Christian living as Jesus expects him to really stands out.

Even so, Christianity may actually help you make friends. True, your love for God may make others think you're weird. But your love for people may convince them that you're not. If your actions and words show that you care about others as much as you care about yourself, not everyone will call you *weird*. A lot of them may call you *friend*.

One of them, an expert in the law, tested him [Jesus] with this question: "Teacher, which is the greatest commandment in the Law?" Jesus replied, "Love the Lord your God with all your heart and with all your soul and with all your mind. . . . And the second is like it: Love your neighbor as yourself."

MATTHEW 22:35–39

14

Mess Up Their Minds

Mike and Trevor were hard at work caddying when they reached the fourteenth hole of the golf course. They walked ahead on the fairway a couple hundred yards to spot balls. When their golfers hit, they stepped behind some trees to wait.

Mike teed up half a dozen golf balls from his golfer's bag and pulled out a big wood to hit them.

"What are you doing?!" Trevor whispered.

"What does it look like I'm doing?" Mike turned to concentrate on his stance. "I . . . *whack* . . . hate . . . *whack* . . . this . . . *whack* . . . guy . . . *whack* . . . so bad . . . *whack whack*." The balls flew off. Then Mike pulled a spare pair of golf gloves out of the bag and tucked them into his pockets. "That's because he tips bad."

Mike and Trevor didn't like the men they were working for. When the men missed a shot, they cussed at Mike and Trevor. Mike's golfer even threw clubs at him.

📩 **Read Romans 12:17–21. What should Mike and Trevor have done? What would you do?**

When someone mistreats you—slugs you or pranks you or says stuff behind your back—your first responsibility is to "do what is right" and "live at peace with

41

everyone." Rather than getting even, try to fix the situation peacefully. The person you're battling with may make peace impossible, but you shouldn't.

If things don't change, leave revenge to God. Here's why: If you want revenge from a sense of fairness, God promises to repay wrong better than you ever can. If you want revenge because you think it will put an end to the situation, think again. Taking revenge on someone who hurts you only prolongs and intensifies the fight. They'll slam you back. Then you'll have to slam them back even worse—and on and on.

"The best way to get rid of an enemy," wrote F. F. Bruce, "is to turn him into a friend." If you want to get back at someone and really mess up his mind, love him. Help him. Be kind to him. That's the only hope you have of disarming him and getting him on your side.

Do not take revenge, my friends, but leave room for God's wrath, for it is written: "It is mine to avenge; I will repay," says the Lord. On the contrary: "If your enemy is hungry, feed him; if he is thirsty, give him something to drink. In doing this, you will heap burning coals on his head." Do not be overcome by evil, but overcome evil with good.

ROMANS 12:19–21

15

Roadkills

You've no doubt studied this phenomenon in science class: When it's time for animals to die, they instinctively do an astonishing thing. Whether furry woodland creatures or city squirrels or bunnies, they mosey quietly to the side of a road, lie down, peacefully take one last breath, and expire.

Wrong. Those animals wander onto the road and get hit by cars. They're called "roadkills."

The sight of a beautiful animal dead on the side of a road is sickening. Just as sad is seeing someone flattened by carelessly spoken words.

Roadkills happen when a driver moves so fast that he strikes an animal before he can stop. Our words kill when we speak without thinking so that we hit someone before we reach the brakes.

Sometimes we don't even bother to brake. We think ahead of time of nasty things to say so that our listeners will think we're cool or funny. That's as bad as gunning the engine.

Now, if we deliberately ran down animals, the courts would take away our driver's license. Unfortunately, no one is going to take away our tongues and lips. We have to learn self-control. All we can do is practice being "quick to listen, but slow to speak" (James 1:19).

Read Ephesians 4:29—5:4. How do we know what is okay to say and what isn't?

Words should be helpful, not harmful. Joking about people isn't helpful. Neither are sexual jokes, either for our minds or for showing others respect. If you say something negative, it should be to build up, not rip down. That means talking directly to the person, not behind his or her back (Matthew 18:15). Using "God" as a swear word means we don't take God seriously. Complaining says we don't like what God has given us, so Paul tells us to give thanks instead.

One other guideline. Just because an animal walks across the road doesn't mean you can hit it. Just because something is true doesn't mean you should say it.

Slow down and let someone live.

———————

Do not let any unwholesome talk come out of your mouths, but only what is helpful for building others up according to their needs, that it may benefit those who listen.

EPHESIANS 4:29

44

16
Playing Keepaway
With the Truth

Dad eyeballs you and your sister as you squirm on the couch. One of you made a bunch of calls to a 900 number, and your dad just opened the whopper bill. Both of you deny it. One of you is lying. Your dad has to figure out who.

Telling a lie is like playing keepaway with a friend's shoe. She needs her shoe back, but you hide it behind your back or toss it over her head, around her side, anywhere that's out of reach. You have fun; after a while your friend who can't get her shoe back grows angry and frustrated. It's hard to go anywhere or do anything with only one shoe.

Read Ephesians 4:20–25. Why is telling the truth important?

Lies never seem so bad when you're the one telling them. After all, liars escape consequences (if you lie to parents or teachers), skip studying (if you cheat on a test), or avoid paying (if you shoplift, or copy tapes or software).

But those benefits are deceitful. When people play games with truth the world grinds to a halt, just like when you can't get a shoe back. When people lie to you, it's hard to know what to believe or whom to trust, who's a winner or who's a loser, who deserves a reward or who deserves punishment, what's good or what's bad, who your friends are or who wants to hurt you. It's hard to live in a world where people lie to you—the shoe of truth you need in order to get on with life keeps flying over your head, out of reach.

You don't like being lied to, so don't lie to others. That's what Ephesians means when it says, "Speak truth, because you are members of one body." Truth is so important to the way the world works that God groups lying with sins most people would never do, like murder, sexual immorality, satanism, and idolatry (Revelation 22:15).

Playing keepaway with the truth never wins.

Therefore each of you must put off falsehood and speak truthfully to his neighbor, for we are all members of one body.

EPHESIANS 4:25

17
Butchered Haircuts

"I guess it means that if I'm going to tell people I'm a Christian, I should act like one," Mark told his youth group. Toward the end of the semester, Mark had cut a class he hated. His teacher had found out, though, and reminded Mark how earlier in the year he had protested having to read a book that seemed anti-Christian. "I really blew it with Mr. Wallace," Mark said. "He called me a hypocrite. He's right. I can't stand up for Jesus one day and act as if I don't know Him the next."

It's ironic. Mark didn't respect a person in authority, and it was that same person who pointed out an inconsistency in his life, a place where he needed to grow.

☑ **Read Romans 13:1–5. Why did God invent authority?**

Paul is blunt. He says that those who rebel against earthly authority rebel against God, and that God will judge them. But he also explains why.

Paul doesn't claim that parents, teachers, coaches, police, bosses, pastors, youth group leaders and other authorities are perfect, or that their judgments are flawless. He does say that God uses authorities to help you, and because of that, he expects you to obey them.

God gives authorities power over you to keep you in

line and to shape your character—even the librarian who yells at you for whispering and for leaning back in your chair, the coach who benches you for sassing back, or the teacher who gives you a bad grade when you don't study. They teach you to respect others' rights, to work as a team and to discipline yourself.

Submitting to authority hurts, but it produces results. Hebrews 12:11 says that "no discipline seems pleasant at the time, but painful. Later on, however, it produces a harvest of righteousness and peace for those who have been trained by it."

When you don't submit to authority, you're like a little kid running from a haircut. God uses authorities like scissors and combs and razors to make you look your best. The more you wiggle, the worse your hair turns out—and the more the process hurts.

Do you want to be free from fear of the one in authority? Then do what is right and he will commend you. For he is God's servant to do you good.

ROMANS 13:3–4

18
Nerd Magnet

Sally calls herself "the nerd magnet." Wherever she goes, she attracts people who aren't quite normal—you know, nerds. For some reason, nerds know Sally won't push them away like other people do. That raises a disturbing question. Do Christians have to be nice to everyone?

"Favoritism" is judging people and being nice (or nasty) to them based on outward appearances.

📝 **Read James 2:1–9. How do James's readers show favoritism?**

In James's story the rich man received polite words and a cushy seat. The poor man got gruff orders to sit on the floor or stand in the back. That was more than a social boo-boo. James writes, "What are you doing? You are making some people more important than others, and with evil thoughts you are deciding that one person is better. . . . You are sinning" (NCV).

James adds that it's foolish to favor the popular while insulting the nerds. The world is like a tree—the most popular, wealthy, athletic, best looking and best dressed sit in the branches way at the top, and the nerds hang out at the bottom.

It's normal to want to climb higher. But people at

the top of the tree try to keep you from climbing into their nest by dropping sticks on your head, kicking your fingers and laughing when you slip and plummet toward the ground. James says they "exploit" you—they use and abuse you. They ridicule your faith. So why show them favoritism?

The people in the bottom branches are special to God, however. Because they have less wealth or looks or popularity, they are often more hungry for God.

From your point of view, a person you thought was a nerd may make a great friend. He (or she) will like you and let you be yourself. You will discover that he's a *person*, not any more weird than you. (And if you do befriend someone and find out he really does have problems, you can point him to where there is help.)

Christlike love respects everyone, not just a favored few. It isn't wrong to show kindness to people who dazzle you. But it's sin if you don't show the same kindness to those who don't.

My brothers, as believers in our glorious Lord Jesus Christ, don't show favoritism. . . . If you really keep the royal law found in Scripture, "Love your neighbor as yourself," you are doing right.

JAMES 2:1, 8

19

Slamming the Dumpster Lid

Matt was tossing trash into the dumpsters behind his apartment when he spotted a stack of *Playboys* under the garbage. Why not take a look?

Mind garbage—it's everywhere. TV shows, videos, music, computer games, magazines, books—a lot like open dumpsters, inviting us to dive in and play.

Some filth is easy to recognize, but some is "I-don't-think-it's-so-bad" dirt we don't notice even when its stench suffocates us—the swimsuit issues and soap operas that warp our view of love and sex, the stars who make us feel less than normal if we don't imitate their fads and morals, the peeks at the rich and famous that cause in us an unscratchable itch to have more and more stuff. Movies and TV dramas can make violence and anger seem like good ways to get things done, and ads often train us to be bored by everything. (Life is seldom as exciting as the frolicking fun of beer ad beach parties, or as electric as soft-drink commercials.)

And all these images seem to say life is happier and easier with God out of the picture. When was the last time God showed up in a commercial?

It takes a lot of guts to slam the dumpster lid shut and go play somewhere else—to switch channels, listen to a different group, find a different video, change magazines—but that's what the Bible urges us to do.

☞ Read Philippians 4:6–8. What should we be watching and listening to and thinking about?

Anything that is good, praiseworthy, true, honorable, right, pure, beautiful and respected—that is what should fill our minds. Read those words again. How much of what we read—and listen to—and think about—during a day passes those tests? What are we doing to slam the lid shut on things that don't, and to open ourselves up to things that do?

No sane person spends his day playing in a real dumpster. Lots of people, though, play in mind garbage, often pulled in by the need for friends, for an escape, for some excitement. The first part of the passage tells us to entrust all our needs to God in prayer. He will meet our needs in a healthy way, and give us a peace that will help us quit playing with mind garbage.

———————

Finally, brothers, whatever is true, whatever is noble, whatever is right, whatever is pure, whatever is lovely, whatever is admirable—if anything is excellent or praiseworthy—think about such things.

PHILIPPIANS 4:8

20

The Belching Llamgod

Shhhh—listen to the pagan drumbeat: BOOM-boom-boomp. BOOM-boom-boomp. Fiery lights flash from the Temple of the Llamgod as worshipers travel well-worn paths crisscrossing the dark jungle.

Worshipers devote hour after hour to accumulating sacrificial offerings before entering the temple gates. Without a sacrifice, worshipers can only wander the edges of the temple, adoring from a distance the temple riches and longing for the day they can charge into the frenzy at the Temple of the Llamgod. The temple attracts many young worshipers, who often slave in the kitchens of the Temple of the Llamgod to prepare lavish offerings.

At the temple, worshipers lay their offerings on ceremonial tables where their gifts are recorded. In return, worshipers receive gaudy trinkets as proof of their sacrifice. Oddly, the trinkets often lose their luster once removed from the temple grounds.

The drums summon worshipers daily, whipping up devotion that even rises in pitch during special seasons at the Temple of the Llamgod.

If a mall (llam) belched smoke or had an idol in the center court, it wouldn't be so hard to see that it can be a temple to a deceptive god: money.

☛ Read 1 Timothy 6:6–10 and 17–19. What should you think about money?

A mall's lights, colors, music, food, friends, and nice stuff stir excitement. They're fun, like the marketplaces in Bible times where people mingled and Jesus and other kids no doubt played.

But when scoping, snaring, and not sharing mall goodies controls your time, affection, and energy, your favorite mall has stolen your heart away from God and other important things. Then the mall has become a temple for enlarging your greed, not a place where you shop to meet your needs. Do the things you buy fit God's plans, or are you standing in line to sacrifice to the Llamgod?

But if we have food and clothing, we will be content with that. People who want to get rich fall into temptation and a trap and into many foolish and harmful desires that plunge men into ruin and destruction.

1 TIMOTHY 6:8–9

21
Step by Step

"Sure, I go to church," Jackie fired back. "Got a problem with that?" Kids had asked Jackie about God a couple of times before, and when she hadn't been able to answer their questions, they laughed. So this time she came out fighting.

Acting like a cornered dog that barks and bites to escape is one response to people confronting your faith—to kids grilling you, teachers asserting opinions you disagree with, maybe a non-Christian parent telling you to spend less time at church. Another reaction is hiding your faith—changing the subject or changing your behavior to fit your surroundings. Either way, fears crash in: *Will I lose this friend? I should know what to say. Shouldn't I stand up for God?*

☑ **Read 1 Peter 3:13–17. How should you respond to people who question your faith?**

Peter encourages you to be unafraid, because Christ is Lord. *Jesus* deserves your deepest awe and obedience. Your first concern should be what *He* thinks, not what others think. Besides, if you can stop your fears from ringing in your ears, you'll be able to hear the Holy Spirit help you know what to say, and when to speak (Mark 13:11).

Nothing beats real love, the example of a changed life, and simple sharing, for demonstrating that God is real. God isn't looking for loud classroom debates, but for gentleness and respect. He doesn't require a big show, but a pure heart—"a clear conscience" that silences lies people say about you.

When Peter says to be prepared to explain your faith, that sounds like a small step for Peter, a giant leap for you. But God will help you take little steps. Ask Him for courage, then start by refusing to hide that you go to church, or to duck when a Christian friend waves "hi" at school. Another step might be bowing your head to silently say a quick thanks for lunch. (Most school lunches need prayer anyway.) Then work on inviting a close friend to church. Practicing the little steps gives you the experience you need to take bigger steps, like speaking up about Jesus to that friend, or to others.

Always be prepared to give an answer to everyone who asks you to give the reason for the hope that you have. But do this with gentleness and respect, keeping a clear conscience, so that those who speak maliciously against your good behavior in Christ may be ashamed of their slander.

1 Peter 3:15–16

22
Being Good in a Bad World

You jab your friends. This is the best part of the movie. The alien being from Planet Zorgon IV is oozing out of town toward the mother ship, having eaten a small but nice town in southern Minnesota. The town's lone survivor aims the nuclear photon ray bazooka he rigged from cornstalks and a rusty muffler—something he learned watching MacGyver on cable. The alien is toast. One shot and it explodes into a gazillion globs—until the sequel, anyway.

You and your friends sigh and leave the theater, relieved that evil has been crushed. After your eyes get used to the light outside, you realize your bikes are gone, ripped off during the movie.

In the real world, evil isn't terminated within ninety minutes, like in a movie. It leaves you wondering if God cares at all about stopping evil.

📭 **Read Malachi 3:13—4:3. What did the people conclude about being good in a bad world?**

The people in the book of Malachi watched evil neighbors get everything good in life, and figured it was useless to keep serving God. They noticed the same things you see every day: cheaters getting A's, drug dealers getting rich, snotty girls getting all the trendy clothes and all the cute guys.

The believers coped by reminding one another that the success of bad people isn't the whole story. In God's judgment at the end of time, evildoers will be punished, but those who follow God will romp like frisky calves set free from their pen. Jesus himself (the "sun of righteousness") will heal believers so that they forget they were ever hurt or discouraged.

So it isn't that God doesn't notice wrongs, or that He doesn't feel your pain. Just the opposite—that's why He sent Christ, to end evil; to give people a chance to turn to Him. However, God is patient and holds off His scorching punishment (2 Peter 2:9; 3:9).

That doesn't mean you relax and tolerate evil. Change what you can in your life and all around you. Work together with other teens and parents and authorities to confront larger evils like drugs and abortion and poverty. But when you feel overcome by evil, you can be patient, reminding yourself that God sees you and won't forget your faithfulness.

But for you who revere my name, the sun of righteousness will rise with healing in its wings. And you will go out and leap like calves released from the stall. Then you will trample down the wicked.

MALACHI 4:2–3

23
Attitude Check

Shivering with fright in the corner of a closet, you wonder *Will they find me?* Big men rip open the door and drag you out. They toss you in the back of a truck, then into a rough cargo plane for a jarring ride to a jungle hideout. Finally the men make it clear that either you will work long days in the hot sun or you will starve. Attitude check: How glad would you be to serve those men?

▶ **Read Exodus 21:1–7. Why does the slave stay with his master?**

People usually become slaves because they have no choice. In Bible times people sold themselves or their children to pay back money they owed. Not long ago Africans were brutalized and forced to serve against their wills.

Exodus 21 shows a slave who said no to freedom so he could stay with his master. His master took the slave to a doorpost and pierced the slave's ear. (Don't try that at home. Your mom won't like a hole in the doorframe.) Piercing the ear showed that the slave was forever his "bondservant," someone who serves a master because he *wants* to.

Crazy? The bondservant didn't think so. He wanted

to work hard for his master because he was thankful for what the master had given him—security, love, a family, food, a home.

In the Bible, Paul often called himself a bondservant of Jesus Christ (one example is in Romans 1:1). Paul was so sure of God's love that he chose to obey God in every way he knew. Paul knew that unlike human masters, God is a righteous and good master. God gives us "every good and perfect gift" (James 1:17), from life itself to His never-ending love.

God isn't a drug lord who twists our arms to make us serve Him, or a slave-master who beats us into submission. He earns our respect, trust and love. Once we're sure that God loves us and wants the best for us, then it's not so crazy—or so hard—to love Him back. We obey Him because we want to, not because we have to.

———

But if the servant declares, "I love my master and my wife and children and do not want to go free," then his master must take him before the judges. He shall take him to the door or the doorpost and pierce his ear with an awl. Then he will be his servant for life.

EXODUS 21:5–6

PART 3

Putting a Lid on PEER FEAR

24
Price Tags

It's a fad in some places to leave price tags dangling from hats and jackets. How handy. That way there's no doubt about whose clothes are more expensive.

How many times a day do you compare "price tags" with someone else? Comparisons often go beyond checking how much our clothes cost. We compare *people* and judge how much they're worth.

Some kids' price tags say that they're almost worthless. There's the kid who sits three seats behind you in math class. Everyone figures he's the dumbest person in your grade. Or you might join your friends when they laugh at Shawna when her unemployed dad drives up in a junker car.

Other people's tags are so expensive that they make *you* feel like a clearance sale leftover. Certain cliques won't let you in because you fall short of their standards. Kids in phy ed class who are more developed than you may make you wonder if you'll ever grow up. Or your youth group might look so spiritual that you doubt you could ever matter to God.

God puts a different price on people.

▶ **Read 1 Peter 1:18–19. How much did God pay for you?**

God thinks that compared to you, even gold is worthless. When God wanted to reestablish a friendship with you, the price that God paid was the death of His Son, Jesus. Cash registers can't count that high! Yet that's the price tag God puts on you and everyone else on earth. That's how much He thinks you're worth. That means no one should ever be tagged as a reject, and you should never feel that way about yourself.

Everyone is equally valuable to God. No one is on sale. No one is an ugly shirt with six markdowns on his price tag that says, "You're worthless. No one wants you." Your price tag says the same thing as all the others in the world: *Jesus loves me and died for me.*

You were bought, not with something that ruins like gold or silver, but with the precious blood of Christ, who was like a pure and perfect lamb.

1 PETER 1:18–19, NCV

25

Looking Good

Sarah frowned at her bedroom mirror. *Jab, lift* with the pick. *Tug, tweak* with a brush. *Fwoosh, fwoosh* with the hairspray. Then for the seventh time that morning Sarah ran into the bathroom to wet down her hair so she could start all over. After all, her bangs didn't *poof* just right.

Even if the whole world were blind, you wouldn't go out in public unwashed and wearing a trash bag. Face it: You primp not just to stay clean and healthy and to feel okay about yourself but to please others. You think you look good only when others think you look good. And guys worry as much as girls. They just worry about other things, like building whomping thighs, massive chests, and peaked biceps.

Some people *will* judge you by your looks. Your task is to decide how much you will let their view of you run your life.

☑ **Read 1 Samuel 16:1–13. What was God looking for in a king for Israel?**

Samuel wanted that kingly look—maybe a face fit for TV. God told Samuel, "Don't look at the outside. That isn't where I look. I check out the inside. I want to see a heart that is good, one that follows me." God picked David, the youngest brother, to be king. David, it turned out, wasn't ugly. However, his tanned, fit appearance showed more than anything that he worked hard at his job as a shepherd.

Looking good matters some. Just remember: The ugliest people in the world are the ones who have perfected their outsides but neglected their insides. God—and people who are really worth impressing—know that your love for people and heart for God matter *more* than what you look like. God doesn't ask, "Did your hair turn out? Are your muscles gargantuan?" What He wants to know is: "Do you work hard? Can your parents trust you? Do you have a good attitude? Are you kind?"

That doesn't mean you should trash your wardrobe and stop washing your hair. God created you and wants you to take care of yourself. But He made you to please Him, not to be a slave to workouts and blow dryers.

The Lord does not look at the things man looks at. Man looks at the outward appearance, but the Lord looks at the heart.

1 SAMUEL 16:7

26

But I Like Fishsticks

Seventh grader Elmer Anthony Towns cleared his throat into a dozen microphones while flashbulbs popped from every direction. "Hi," he squeaked as reporters jostled for better positions. Then the President of the United States strode to the platform to join Elmer.

"I am proud to award this Medal of Courage to Elmer, or 'Eats,' as his buddies call him," the President said. "As the first middle schooler in our country's history to stand and proclaim that he likes school lunches, he sets an example of courage all America should imitate."

Admitting you like fishsticks will get you almost that much attention.

It's hard to be different. Junior high seems to force everyone to be the same. Short people get pulled up by the hair to proper height, and tall people get their heads mowed off. Everyone has to fit the same mold.

Does God expect you to be like everyone else?

▶ **Read 1 Corinthians 12:12–20.**

God thrives on the variety He built into His creation. Your high points, low points, or anything that makes you stand out from the people around you show that

He made you unique, a one-of-a-kind creation. Be glad you're different from others, because *your* uniqueness plus *their* uniqueness adds up to a stronger whole. To win, a team needs players with a mix of skills. To design, make, and sell a product, a business needs a variety of gifts. To grow together like a body, the church—and your school, in fact—needs you to contribute your unique gifts and personality. So don't be ashamed to be yourself.

It's not worth inviting mob ridicule by standing on your lunchroom seat to shout that you like the school's food better than your mom's. There are bigger things to stand firm for—being friends with someone unpopular, enjoying a class besides phy ed, not doing sex or drugs or alcohol, liking your parents or being proud to be a Christian. Those are a few differences worth defending.

If the whole body were an eye, where would the sense of hearing be? If the whole body were an ear, where would the sense of smell be? But in fact God has arranged the parts in the body, every one of them, just as he wanted them to be.

1 CORINTHIANS 12:17–18

27

I Was Here

The note left on the lunch table read: *"I was here. Did you even notice?"*

Feeling unnoticed, average, and expendable is no fun. It's like being invisible. Being so-so at sports means better players get all the attention. Doing average at school means neither teachers nor tutors notice you. Being your age—not a kid, not an adult—guarantees that some people will ignore you. Having really smart brothers or sisters can make you feel worthless to your family. It makes you wish you could change your looks, age, clothes, personality, talents, brains—anything to break loose from the crowd to feel unique and important!

Jeremiah was a teenaged shepherd known to no one when God called him to preach.

📝 **Read Jeremiah 1:4–10. How did Jeremiah respond to God when God told him to speak up?**

Jeremiah probably thought his sheep could do better for God. He reminded God that he was a nobody, young and fumble-mouthed.

God didn't see Jeremiah that way. He wanted to use the young shepherd to challenge the kings and people of Israel with a piercing message. God told Jeremiah that He had made plans for his life even before he was born.

Jeremiah was anything but ordinary when God got through with him. God transformed him from a scared shepherd to a gutsy prophet. What made Jeremiah useful to God wasn't his abilities or lack of them, but his obedience to God's plan. Piles of people are talented and smart. Few are like Jeremiah: obedient and available to God.

God chooses and uses ordinary people so that everyone will realize that skills and abilities and talents are gifts from God (1 Corinthians 1:26–31). Whether or not you stand out in a crowd isn't what makes you matter. It's having an obedient heart that lets God lead you in the unique plan He's crafted for you.

But the Lord said to me, "Do not say, 'I am only a child.' You must go to everyone I send you to and say whatever I command you. Do not be afraid of them, for I am with you and will rescue you," declares the Lord.

JEREMIAH 1:7–8

28
The Spotlight

"It's a long fly ball," Cory bellowed in a sportscaster voice as Vinnie rounded first base. "The big V really smashed that one! What power! What grace!" Cheers were buried by laughter and the smash hit forgotten, however, as Vinnie tripped over second base and skidded in the dirt, shredding his knees.

Some days you might think you'll never do any better than Vinnie.

But you won't always fall on your face. Sooner or later—maybe just in little ways—you'll see the crowd, hear the applause, bask in the spotlight. You might score the highest in your class, grow up into a hunk or a beauty queen some summer, or sweat hard and finally make the basketball team. You might discover a hobby or a job you excel at.

Applause is fun. Compliments make you feel good. But they can also make you a nasty person who looks down on people, ignores old friends and expects special treatment.

When things go well and people applaud, how do you keep from becoming a snob?

☑ **Read Philippians 2:3–8. How did Jesus practice humility?**

Jesus sought servanthood, not the spotlight. If anyone ever had a right to applause, it was Jesus. He's

God! He possessed the majesty and splendor of the King of the universe, yet He didn't draw attention to himself. Instead of rolling up in a limo and making a big splash, He came quietly as a helpless baby and grew up to be a servant who died on the cross for the sins of His creation.

When the glare of the spotlight blinds you, you only see yourself. You can fight that temptation to think only of yourself by stepping out of the spotlight, like Jesus, through servanthood. Run away from selfishness by remembering other people's needs as much as your own.

You can also share the spotlight with your Lord. After all, God is the real source of your gifts, talents, and abilities (1 Corinthians 4:7). When people applaud you, applaud God! Tell Him thanks for your success, and remember that He is more important than anything you achieve (Jeremiah 9:23–24).

Do nothing out of selfish ambition or vain conceit, but in humility consider others better than yourselves. Each of you should look not only to his own interests, but also to the interests of others. Your attitude should be the same as that of Christ Jesus.

PHILIPPIANS 2:3–5

29

Loves Me Not

You signed up for German because you thought the girl you like would take it, but she took Spanish. So you suffer through a teacher who spits on you when she says "Ich liebe dich." Pluck a flower and it would slap you *She loves me not. She loves me not.*

Or you're a girl and the guy you adore from afar changes girlfriends quicker than you can change TV channels. He "goes with" a dozen girls a month. Never you. *He loves me not.*

Rejection—the person you like doesn't like you back. You wonder: *What's wrong with me?* You worry: *Everyone thinks I'm a loser.* You wallow in the unspeakable: *I'll spend my life as a nun.*

☑ **Read James 1:16–17. What does God have to do with finding someone for you?**

God intends for most people to get married (1 Corinthians 7). That's probably what He plans for you. So the question most likely isn't *if* you'll find someone but *when* and *who.*

James says that "every good and perfect gift is from above." God knows what you need when you need it. You can trust Him to give you the right gift at the right time, whether it's your driver's license, a date, or your first real kiss.

That doesn't mean God doesn't care about right now. He feels your rejection more than you can ever imagine, because He was rejected by the people He made (John 1:10–11). It's just that God's best gift to you might also be *not* letting you go with that guy or girl—or *anyone*—right now. Dating too soon or dating the wrong person messes up your other relationships and responsibilities. And it can make it harder to keep sex for marriage.

God sees your whole life. He wants you to be ready for a marriage devoted to Him, not just to find you someone for the party this Friday. The gift you want Him to drop on you is a quick date, but the gift He gives is patience, character—and, at the right time, almost for sure—trust Him—the right mate.

Every good and perfect gift is from above, coming down from the Father of heavenly lights, who does not change like shifting shadows.

JAMES 1:17

30

On the Couch

Derek had kissed Ericka awkwardly on the cheek and she kissed him back. Then he wanted to touch her in ways that made her feel both uncomfortable and yet excited. Now neither of them knows what to do! She's never been so close to a boy or felt so loved. She likes Derek's warm attention. And he wants to keep kissing her—maybe more than that.

After a nervous minute Derek suddenly blurts out, "I really like you a lot." Ericka is thrilled to hear those words, but wonders what they mean.

Freeze frame: Is love the reason why Derek and Ericka are kissing on the couch?

Doubtful. Ericka enjoys Derek's affection, which makes her feel as pretty as the other girls she knows. To keep him liking her, she's willing to do things she probably wouldn't do otherwise. She's using Derek. But Derek is using Ericka, too. Having a girlfriend shows him and his friends he's not gay or a whuss. Going as far as he can with her makes things even more sure.

Read Proverbs 5:15–23, which talks about God's awesome plan for sex.

Proverbs compares sex and love to water. In a desert, only a madman would carelessly spill the water he needs to survive. Marriage is God's way to protect sexual love as the priceless treasure God made it to be. Love in marriage is for each other, not to look good for others. Ericka won't worry about Derek leaving, and Derek can be good to Ericka, not just get what he can. Real love between a man and a woman is million-dollar stuff, but Ericka and Derek are trashing it like it's worth pennies by letting what others think determine their behavior.

But Ericka and Derek weren't having sex. And junior highers aren't ready for marriage. What about kisses and hugs? When are they okay?

They aren't meant to be spilled all over, either, because they're meant to lead to more. They're part of love, like a good warm-up band before the main concert.

Your parents (and youth pastor or other Christian adults you trust) can help you *set and keep* limits that will stop you from wasting one of God's best inventions. If your parents didn't understand the feelings you're facing as you grow up, you wouldn't be here! Proverbs 6:20–27 says to "keep your father's commands and don't forget your mother's teaching." Talk to them.

Be faithful to your own wife, just as you drink water from your own well. Don't pour your water in the streets; don't give your love to just any woman. These things are yours alone and shouldn't be shared with strangers.

PROVERBS 5:15–17, NCV

76

31
It's Funny Until You Put an Eye Out

With dual dartguns set to shoot, Andrew charged from behind the couch, put a dartgun on each side of Nick's head and pulled the triggers. *Fwank, Thunk!* Andrew laughed as he retreated to reload while Nick faked pain. Then from the living room came a yell that halted the dartgun war: "It's funny until you put an eye out! Stop it right now."

We ignore rules that we think are too harsh: "Cross the street only at crosswalks." "Don't run in the hall." "Don't shoot dartguns at people's heads." Breaking those rules doesn't always carry the big bad consequences the rulemakers seem to threaten, so we take our chances and do what we want.

Some people treat God's rules the same way, ignoring His warnings about right and wrong because they think they're for someone else, or too hard or too old-fashioned to be obeyed. On top of that, they ignore you, laugh at you when you take God seriously and don't join their activities.

☑️ **Read Psalm 119:89–96. What makes God worth obeying? Why not listen to someone else?**

For starters, it doesn't hurt to remember that God spoke and created heaven and earth, so He gets to make the rules and set consequences for breaking them. We can choose to ignore some rules in life, but not God's.

But there are more reasons to obey—and to laugh back at those who laugh at you—than the fact that God can roast His enemies. God is loving and smart. Of all the rulemakers in your world, only God puts together earth-shaking power, flawless wisdom, and total love. The result? Perfect judgment about what's right and what's wrong, what builds up and what rips down. Not one of His rules is dumb or out-of-date, and not a single one is meant for anything less than your good.

That's what God's "faithfulness" is all about. People's nastiness won't destroy you if you grasp the perfection of God's ways—His "laws," "precepts," "statutes," and "commands." Threats, teasing, and laughter loom over you only until you see their puniness compared to God's boundless wise care.

If your law had not been my delight, I would have perished in my affliction.

PSALM 119:92

32
Snow Forts

"You can't come in here, runt," Angie scowled. "Go build your own fort." Her little brother trudged through the snow to the far side of their yard. He built his own snow fort and sulked in it by himself. He packed hard snowballs that froze into ice balls to lob at his sister and her friends.

Isn't Angie's fort just like a clique?

If you live where it snows, it's great to build a snow fort. If you build thick walls and a roof, you can stay warm even if it's cold enough to kill outside. Just like that, a clique can be good. Cold winds of insecurity, peer pressure, hormones, and potential for failure blow through the world of junior high. In a clique, you and your friends can stick together for warmth.

But a clique is cold agony if you're on the outside. You freeze to death because the clique won't let you in. Like a snow fort, a clique is toasty on the inside and freezing on the outside.

📩 **Read 1 John 4:7–12. If God built a snow fort, what would it be like?**

God's snow fort is the group of people who believe in Jesus Christ. He has only one entrance requirement: friendship with Christ. God doesn't ice out people from the wrong school or neighborhood, or people who dress wrong or who aren't quite cool, pretty or popular enough.

God's snow fort can't ever get too crowded. He keeps ripping down walls and building rooms. He's always inviting more people in.

The only problem comes when people inside the fort decide they won't let any more people in. First John 4:19 says we can include people in our group because God has included us—we can love because He has loved us. That isn't always comfy. We may have to squish to let someone else in, but that's what makes God's snow fort different from Angie's.

So stay warm with your friends. That's great. But remember to welcome others in from the cold.

Dear friends, let us love one another, for love comes from God. Everyone who loves has been born of God and knows God. Whoever does not love does not know God, because God is love. This is how God showed his love among us: He sent his one and only Son into the world that we might live through him.

1 JOHN 4:7–9

33

No-Stick Jesus

Jennifer whirled around and pretended to dig in the bottom of her locker. Her long hair hid her wet eyes. She didn't want anyone to see her cry. *ZITFACE!* echoed in her head. *How could Ashley say that about me?* she thought. *She's supposed to be my friend. Everyone in the stupid hall heard!*

Jennifer walked home from school that day instead of taking the bus. She cut through some backyards so Ashley couldn't look out from her house across the street and see her walking alone. That night she lay in bed rehearsing all the things she wished she had said.

Sticks and stones may break our bones, but being called names hurts even worse. We're Teflon people. Food is supposed to slip right out of those coated pans, but it never works that easy. Careless cooks scratch Teflon; then it doesn't work too well. In the same way, careless people scratch us, and insults that are supposed to slide off stick and stink like burnt food on Teflon. We can't shake off the insults: *You're ugly. You're dumb. You'll never get a girlfriend. You'll never make the team.* Those words hurt. Like the Bible says, "Reckless words pierce like a sword" (Proverbs 12:18).

But Jesus had a way of letting what people said slide right off.

☑ **Read 1 Peter 2:21–25. How did Jesus react to put-downs?**

Jesus didn't insult in return—that would make Him as bad as His tormentors.

Instead, He trusted the Father who sees perfectly. He realized one opinion counted more than all of the others put together. Do the people who shred you know you? Not as well as God does. Is what people say true? If you actually do have something wrong with you, God tells you constructively—with great timing, gently, helping you change.

Next time someone insults you, let it slip off by listening instead to what God says about you. You're His daughter or son. He loves you more than anyone else does. Listen for *God's* evaluation of your words, dress, looks, attitudes, actions, sins, faults, and skills. It's God's opinion that counts.

———————

When they hurled their insults at him [Jesus], he did not retaliate; when he suffered, he made no threats. Instead, he entrusted himself to him who judges justly.

1 PETER 2:23

34

We Are the Champions

Each spring baseball fans predict that year's World Series winner. Who will it be? How can you see the finish? Wishful thinking doesn't win championships—ask any Chicago Cubs' fan. Being picked to win doesn't do it—plenty can go wrong during the season. Buying multimillion dollar players doesn't always work. Trusting luck is a copout—every team gets good and bad breaks.

Baseball fans—and players—would be less uptight about the season if they knew from the start who would win at the end. Of course, knowing the winners ahead of time kills the thrill of sports.

You're at the beginning of the season as far as your life is concerned. How will *you* finish at the end of the season? It isn't much fun wondering how your life will turn out. Are you going to win? How can you tell?

☑ **Read Philippians 1:3–11. What sort of future could the Philippians expect?**

Paul wrote to the Philippians that he was certain about one thing: Because they belonged to God, He would never let them go. He would keep perfecting their faith until the time Christ comes back to earth. At the end of the season, they would be winners.

That wasn't just a happy wish. Paul had seen God start His work in the Philippians. They had become believers and had begun to spread the good news about Jesus Christ. As they continued as Paul's partners, God's life grew in them. Because God keeps all His promises, even suffering and death could not rip victory out of their hands (1:22, 29).

Some days you'll feel like a batter in an endless slump in the game of life. You may feel like a social reject, unlikable, ugly, awful at everything. God will coach you out of those slumps. What's more, His eternal game plan means that even though you don't always win in those things, you'll win big at the end of the season in what matters the very most: your relationship with God. If you let God be your coach, He promises to make you a spiritual champion.

Being confident of this, that he who began a good work in you will carry it on to completion until the day of Christ Jesus.

PHILIPPIANS 1:6

35

Phlegmwad

Andre sat alone at the lunch table, glancing around for a friendly face. A group of older girls came over, called him a phlegmwad and said that he was getting their section slimy. He was new at school, but took that as a hint he should move. He didn't mind so much because he had spotted Dan, a kid he recognized from math class.

Dan didn't look too barbaric, and Andre thought he had a good shot at making a new friend. When Andre went over to Dan's table and sat down, though, everyone ignored him. Andre ate his lunch next to Dan and his friends, but he felt even more lonely than when he had been alone.

You don't have to be new at school to feel lonely. When strangers trounce you, your friends act like enemies, or your parents and family don't understand you, you feel isolated, left out. And since you can't see God, even He can seem like He's nowhere near.

☑ **Read Psalm 73:21–28. How did the writer react to loneliness?**

One of King David's musicians, Asaph (AY-saf), wrote Psalm 73 when he felt cut off from everyone around him because he followed God. What he discovered can help your loneliness, whatever the reason.

Asaph expected that God would fix his situation instantly. He no doubt thought that as a follower of God, he was a friend worth having. He should be liked, popular—and included. In time, God surely gave him friends, but for a while God let him be alone.

Asaph found that God sometimes lets you feel lonely to remind you that all you really have is God, and that He is all you need. Family won't always be there—parents have lots to do, and someday you'll move out. Whom will you depend on? Friends move, or you just change. Whom will you hang out with?

In the middle of being lonely Asaph came to a simple conclusion: *God* is always near. When you have no one else, you have God, and He's enough.

Yet I am always with you; you hold me by my right hand. You guide me with your counsel, and afterward you will take me into glory. Whom have I in heaven but you? And earth has nothing I desire besides you. My flesh and my heart may fail, but God is the strength of my heart and my portion forever.

PSALM 73:23–26

PART 4

Digging for the GOOD STUFF

36

God Is the Crust

If life were a pizza, God would be the crust.

Junior highers toss a lot of toppings on their pizza—school, sports, clothes, sleeping, relaxing, shopping, lessons, clubs, parties, and more. God isn't just another topping on the menu you can pick or ignore. Nor can you ask for God on one part of the pizza and leave Him off the rest. You can't slice up your life and say, "These are the pieces without God, and these are the pieces with God—church and youth group."

If Jesus is your Lord and Savior, He's a part of everything you do. He gives your life its shape and determines what fits on top and what doesn't. Without the crust, everything slides off.

Pizza crusts, however, are always in danger of being ignored because the toppings are so obvious. Because you *can't* see God, it's easy to forget Him in the midst of all the things to do that you *can* see. When you eat a pizza, you need to slow down and savor the crust. When you go through your week, you need to slow down and concentrate on God.

📑 **Read Mark 1:35. How did Jesus fix His attention on God?**

You can spend time with God two ways: in a group or by yourself. You need both to grow spiritually. In a group you're encouraged by the strong faith and support of other Christians. Groups allow you to get fired up and celebrate your friendship with God.

Getting alone to be with God helps you get to know God personally, just like you need time one-on-one with someone to really know that person. That's what Jesus did. Even He needed time to talk with God alone.

Reading your Bible—and using books like this one to help you understand the Bible—is part of that. Reading the Bible is how God speaks to you. Learning to talk *to* God—learning to pray—is the other part of spending time with God. God doesn't want to talk *at* you but *with* you.

Very early in the morning, while it was still dark, Jesus got up, left the house and went off to a solitary place, where he prayed.

MARK 1:35

37

What Do You Say to a Star?

Imagine you won a contest to meet a superstar—let's say your favorite actress. Your parents drive you to a gleaming hotel, and two bodyguards with no necks meet you and escort you to the star's room. Other bodyguards push back screaming fans. The door cracks open, you dart in, and you're standing just inches from a celebrity you would give away your best friend to meet. What do you say?

After scraping your jaw off the floor, you would probably hit three themes: "I'm glad to meet you." (You tell her you're happy to be her friend.) "You're the best actress in the whole world." (You tell her she's a great person.) "Your last movie was so cool." (You tell her specific things she does that you like.)

You may wonder what to say to God when you pray. Someone once said that the word PRAY is a reminder of four things to do in prayer: Praise . . . Repent . . . Ask . . . Yield. When you're at a loss for words to pray, *praise* is a great place to start.

☑ **Read Psalm 18:25–36. What sort of things does David praise God for?**

Knowing that you might fumble your words if you met a movie star, you would probably think ahead of time what to say—maybe even write it out. Applauding God with praise might take that kind of practice for you. Just say the same three kinds of things you would say to a star: Express friendship ("God, I'm glad I know you"); worship God for who He is ("You're an awesome God"); and thank God for what He does ("Thanks for helping me get my homework done"). It may help to read passages in the book of Psalms or to learn worship songs to discover what to say.

That might make you squirm, though, if you start to think that praise has to be gushy poetry set to music that makes you gag. Your praise doesn't need to be stiff, elegant, soft or formal. Praise at its simplest is just using your mouth to applaud God, telling Him He's great, whatever that sounds like coming from you. It's words you mean, telling God what you think of Him.

With your help I can advance against a troop; with my God I can scale a wall. As for God, his way is perfect; the word of the Lord is flawless. He is a shield for all who take refuge in him. For who is God besides the Lord? And who is the Rock except our God?.

PSALM 18:29–31

38
Church Is Boring

Whap! Your pastor slaps the pulpit, and the congregation hushes. He always does that when he reaches an important point. Everyone stops rustling and coughing. You could hear a baby breathe in the silence.

The note your best friend passed was unusually funny, so you aren't listening. Your face contorts. The pew shakes. You try to laugh without making any noise. You know you blew it when you notice the silence, look up, and see your parents three rows in front of you turned all the way around, staring at you. Beyond them the pastor glares down at you and your friends with one eyebrow raised. You shut up and start rehearsing your excuse for later: *Church services are so boring. . . .*

Church isn't always fun. It's often designed for adults. It involves learning and correction. But assuming you're not a rebel who wants nothing to do with God or church, a big reason church services are boring is lack of understanding. All you may know about worship and praise is "Get up. Get dressed. Get in the car. Sit still and shut up."

Read Deuteronomy 6:4–9. How do kids learn their parents' faith?

Adults are supposed to explain what being a believer is all about. Some don't—not in a way that helps you. So you need to dig.

For starters, ask your parents what's going on. *Try to understand what's happening in the service.* If you watch a sporting event without knowing the rules, you get bored. At church, if you don't understand who the players are, why you stand or sit, or what the words in the music or sermon mean, you'll shrivel up. If you can follow what's going on, you may learn to like it.

Then ask your parents why they go to church. Why aren't they bored? If you watch a football game on TV all by yourself with the sound turned down, it gets boring. You need to be part of the oomph of the crowd to feel interested. Find out why God is important to your parents. Why did they start going to church? Why do they keep going? Why is worshiping God so crucial that you have to get up, get dressed, get in the car, sit still and shut up?

Love the Lord your God with all your heart and with all your soul and with all your strength. These commandments that I give you today are to be upon your hearts. Impress them on your children.

DEUTERONOMY 6:5–7

39

The First Church of True Believers

Holly, president of the youth group at the First Church of True Believers, strode to the front of the church to pray. "God, ahem. I'm speaking. I thank you that we are not like the teens of this world who take part in sex and drugs. We have Bible studies three evenings a week. We go on summer missions trips. We witness at school. We're just exactly the way you want us to be—not like scum who don't know you." She thumped her Bible—it looked as big as a library dictionary—then she smiled and said, "Amen!"

Andy sat in the back row of the church with his face in his hands. He had slipped in the back pew late after having a whopper fight with his parents. "God, I don't think I can ever be what you want me to be. Please forgive me."

☑ **Read Luke 18:9–14. Who was God happier with, Holly or Andy?**

God doesn't hear your prayers because you've racked up a bunch of points by doing good or not doing bad. God hears you because Christ died and rose for you.

The second ingredient in PRAY is the "R": *Repentance*. Repentance means to admit sin is sin, to not make excuses. If someone is "repentant," it means he comes to God in humility, realizing that he needs forgiveness. God isn't happy with sin. But He's even less happy if we're too proud to admit that we sin against God in what we think, say, and do.

Remember how sin builds a wall between you and God? Asking for forgiveness keeps the wall torn down and communication open. When you pray, take time to remember if there's anything you need to clear up between you and God.

Think how uncomfortable you are talking to your parents if you've done something wrong that they don't know about. You avoid being with your parents or looking at them. You sweat if they start asking questions. But the relationship is repaired as soon as you open up. It's the same with God. The person who hides sin from God is miserable, but the one who admits sin is happy and forgiven (Psalm 32:1–6).

The tax collector stood at a distance. He would not even look up to heaven, but beat his breast and said, "God, have mercy on me, a sinner." I tell you that this man, rather than the other, went home justified before God. For everyone who exalts himself will be humbled, and he who humbles himself will be exalted.

LUKE 18:13–14

96

40

God Is No Grouch

What aggravation! You need help, but the person you ask won't give it—like a teacher who calls your questions stupid, or a friend who puts off working together on a project. How about a store clerk who won't help you find what you need but instead follows you around the store expecting you to shoplift just because of your age? It makes you walk away feeling awful, mumbling to yourself, "Fine. You don't care? I don't need you. I'll do it myself."

Jesus used an example like that to teach about prayer.

✔️ **Read Luke 11:5–13. How does God respond to requests?**

Jesus tells a story about a man who has an unexpected visitor show up at his door in the middle of the night. The host, though obligated to feed the visitor, has nothing to serve. So he bangs on a friend's door to borrow bread. Upset, the friend grouches about the time of night and slams the door. In the end he wears down and gives in, loaning the bread only so he can get rid of his annoying friend and go back to bed.

The "A" in "PRAY" is for "Ask." Part of prayer is asking God to provide for your needs and wants. But why do that if you feel you're bugging God to do something He doesn't want to do?

Jesus wants you to know that God is the exact *opposite* of the midnight grouch—or a belittling teacher, flaky friend, or suspicious clerk. You aren't being a pain to God when you ask Him to meet your needs. In fact, Jesus encourages you to ask, expecting an answer: "Whoever asks, receives."

Jesus uses a bizarre comparison to show God's eagerness to answer your prayers. No father, He says, would give his child a snake instead of a fish, or a scorpion instead of an egg. Jesus' point is that if an earthly father, who sins and makes mistakes, can muster that much compassion, then you can be confident, knowing that your perfect heavenly Father will be unfailing in giving you good gifts.

So I say to you: Ask and it will be given to you; seek and you will find; knock and the door will be opened to you. For everyone who asks receives; he who seeks finds; and to him who knocks, the door will be opened.

LUKE 11:9–10

41

Jesus' Prayer

"O God who reigneth in the heavenlies," Mr. Hannon prayed, "we thank thee for plucking us from the mire of iniquity and designating us your offspring." Translation? "God of the universe, thanks for freeing us from sin and for calling us your children."

People use strange words when they pray, words that they would never use any other time. It can confuse us and lose us, like it did Jesus' disciples. They heard religious leaders pray all the time, but they noticed that Jesus' prayers were different. So they asked Jesus to teach them to pray.

📖 **Read Matthew 6:5–13. What did Jesus tell them?**

He told them not to pray in public just to get attention, and He said long prayers don't get any better response from God than short ones. Then Jesus gave His disciples a sort of pattern to follow. He didn't say "pray these words"—though there's nothing wrong with that—but "pray something like this."

What he taught them (the Lord's Prayer) has several parts: "Our Father in heaven, hallowed be your name." That's praise—saying people should recognize God as holy. "Forgive us our debts, as we forgive our debtors." That's repentance—asking forgiveness for sins.

The other petitions are examples of the "Ask" part of PRAY. Some are spiritual requests. "Your kingdom come, your will be done on earth as it is in heaven" asks that God would rule in our lives and in the world. "Lead us not into temptation" is similar. It asks that God would keep evil from luring us away from Him. Another request is practical. "Give us today our daily bread" is asking for things we need for survival in this world—food, a place to live, clothing, work, help at school, family harmony, and solid friends.

Jesus' sample prayer is *straightforward*, meant for talking with God, not impressing people. His prayer is *sure*; He talks to God as Father, confident of an answer. And His prayer is *simple*. It skips the fancy words and asks straightforwardly for the things we need.

This, then, is how you should pray: "Our Father in heaven, hallowed be your name, your kingdom come, your will be done on earth as it is in heaven. Give us today our daily bread. Forgive us our debts, as we also have forgiven our debtors. And lead us not into temptation, but deliver us from the evil one.

MATTHEW 6:9–13

42
Prayer Abuse

Somewhere in the high channels on your TV, between the shopping networks and the B-movie reruns, there exists the TV Preacher Zone. A few occupants of the zone are honest teachers of the Word of God. Others perpetrate a common crime: prayer abuse. Don't buy what they sell: *Prayer: It will make your dreams come true! Just believe hard enough, use my formula, promise to be good and SHAZAM! God answers every prayer. Think of the possibilities, folks! Get an A on every test, make pimples vanish, always play your violin in tune, and sink every just-as-the-buzzer-sounds shot from half-court. Keep your dog from dying, your parents from fighting, and your best friend from moving away.* Click.

▶ **Read John 15:7–14. Does Jesus agree with the TV preachers?**

Jesus did say, "Ask whatever you wish, and it will be given you." But here's the crucial part: *If* you remain in Him and His words remain in you, *then* God will give what you ask. "To remain" means to be like a vine that stays connected to the branch. If you "remain" you draw life from God, resulting in obedience to God. To have Christ's words in you means you're shaped by His promises, values, and priorities.

That doesn't mean God answers only the prayers of super-spiritual people, or that anyone can earn His favor. It just means that if you live close to God, you'll want what God wants for you, and He'll gladly grant that request. You'll want things that make you more like Christ so you show God's greatness, His glory. That's an incredible promise you can rely on.

Even so, you don't always get what you want, because no one *always* prays perfectly within God's will. Sometimes it's easy to spot prayer abuse—like praying to get a fake ID so you can sneak into an R-rated movie. The book of James is clear about those prayers: You don't get what you ask for because your motives stink (4:3).

Other times you just don't realize you're asking for something God doesn't want for you. And once in a while it won't make any sense to you why God didn't answer a prayer the way you thought He should. That's when you need to remember that only God can see the best possible answer to your every request.

If you remain in me and my words remain in you, ask whatever you wish, and it will be given you. This is to my Father's glory, that you bear much fruit, showing yourselves to be my disciples.

JOHN 15:7–8

43

Lord, You Pick

"No! You can't get a new bike this year," Kyle's dad answered. "Next year."

"All my friends have new ones," Kyle countered. "I don't want to ride my old one anymore. I look like a dork on it." Kyle's dad gave him that look that says "Discussion ended."

The next summer Kyle's dad kept his promise and bought him a new bike. Since Kyle had grown several inches over the winter, Kyle got an awesome adult-sized bike. His friends had grown too, and their new bikes were too small. Now they were the ones who looked funny.

Kyle's dad evaluated whether or not he needed the bike, decided he did, but also knew next year would be better timing. When you ask God for something, He does the same thing. You can't treat God like a cosmic candy machine—put in the right stuff, hit a button and expect the sweet of your choice. In prayer, the final choice is up to God, not you.

"Yield" is the fourth part of PRAY. It means having an attitude that says, "God, answer this as you see best, according to your plan, not mine."

Read Luke 22:39–46. How does Jesus' prayer before He died on the cross show Him yielding to God's choice?

Jesus knew that dying for the world's sins would be more painful than anyone could imagine. He wondered whether there was another way to save the world. So He prayed, "Father, if it is possible, don't let me go through this." But He closed His prayer by leaving the choice to God: "Not my will, but yours be done."

Jesus trusted that His Father knew best. He accepted His Father's answer without complaint. He said to God, "You pick. You decide." He trusted that whatever God's answer was, it would be the best. Not the easiest, not the most comfortable, but the best.

———

He [Jesus] withdrew about a stone's throw beyond them, knelt down and prayed. "Father, if you are willing, take this cup from me; yet not my will, but yours be done."

LUKE 22:41–44

44

Rip a Hole in the Roof

Teresa stood by the door to the girls' locker room after phy ed, looking pale and foggy. A friend spotted her and ran over. "What's wrong?"

"I think I broke my arm." Good conclusion, considering it looked like a piece of hanger art, bent in three new directions. How Teresa managed to slip by the gym teacher no one could figure out, but she was in such a pained daze that her friends had to gently lead her to the school nurse, who called Teresa's parents.

📝 **Read Mark 2:1–12. How did the paralyzed man's friends help him get healed?**

Lots of people you know need help getting to Jesus. Even though Jesus doesn't tour around like He did in the Bible, we can still bring friends to Him through prayer.

Like the paralytic on his stretcher, your friends may not be able to get to Jesus by themselves. They may be sick—too depressed or medicated to pray. Their need may be so big that no human being can handle it alone—like coping with their parents' divorce, a dad's heart attack, or a sibling's suicide. Or the friends, classmates, parents or other people you care about may not even be Christians—and so unaware of their need for Christ and His help that they would never pray for themselves.

Jesus healed the paralytic physically and spiritually. You may not always see those results from your prayers—sometimes God has a better plan. At other times the person you pray for may continue to resist God—like a parent who has an affair and refuses to come home. God would like to fix the situation, but the person won't let Him.

Even so, *your* faith allows God to act among even your non-Christian friends. Your prayers can help a friend get healed, find hope, or become a Christian. God won't force himself on anybody, but praying for your friends is like opening a crack in the door to let God into the situation, or like ripping a hole in the roof and bringing your concerns right to God.

Some men came, bringing to [Jesus] a paralytic, carried by four of them. Since they could not get him to Jesus because of the crowd, they made an opening in the roof above Jesus and, after digging through it, lowered the mat the paralyzed man was lying on.

MARK 2:3—4

45

Prayer Changes Things

The bumper sticker on the car read, "Prayer Changes Things."

But the car didn't look like a reason to believe that prayer works. The beater was twenty-some years old and it coughed black smoke as it rumbled slightly sideways down the highway. Prayer hadn't miraculously gotten that guy a better car, or even a better job so he could get a better car. More than that, a stick figure in a wheelchair on the car's license plate advertised that the car's driver was handicapped. If God answers prayer, why wasn't the driver healed?

Have you or a friend ever prayed and it seemed God didn't hear? You prayed for your parents; they still got divorced. You prayed for your grandparents; they got sick and died. You prayed for a friend; the one who got moved away. Or you prayed for smaller things—good grades, a place on the team, a role in a play—and nothing seemed to happen.

☑ **Read 2 Corinthians 12:7–10, where Paul prayed to God for help dealing with a "thorn in the flesh"—maybe an opponent, maybe an illness. Even though we don't know exactly what Paul's problem was, we know the result. What did prayer change?**

Prayer didn't change Paul's circumstances. It changed Paul.

Paul's problem was so bad that he prayed three times for God to take it away. Finally God said no. But God told Paul He would strengthen him in the middle of his agony.

Paul needed the thorn to keep him from becoming proud of his great spiritual insights. The thorn made him depend on God and realize that God was closest when he struggled. That didn't make the thorn any less painful, but Paul learned that God could use the thorn for good.

When you don't see the answers you want to your prayers, try to see what God is working to develop in you and in your relationship with Him. Prayer *always* changes the person who prays in faith *if* he or she trusts that God hears and cares. Prayer that seems to fail produces a Christian who succeeds.

———————

Three times I pleaded with the Lord to take it away from me. But he said to me, "My grace is sufficient for you, for my power is made perfect in weakness."

2 CORINTHIANS 12:8–9

46

Can You Really Trust This Guy?

He had told them to row to the other side of the lake. It sounded easy enough, but as Jesus' disciples bullied the boat into the wind, they must have thought His command was ridiculous. With oars flexing and hull groaning, the boat drifted backward almost as much as it lurched forward.

In the middle of the night they suddenly saw someone coming toward them. Without a boat. On *top* of the water. It was Jesus, but they didn't know that. They thought it could only be a ghost. Jesus calmed them before their terror could drive them overboard: "Take courage. It is I. Don't be afraid."

📝 **Read Matthew 14:22–33. What did Jesus' disciples learn in the middle of the storm?**

Jesus' stroll on the sea gave His disciples courage. He saw them straining to follow His command (Mark 6:48), and wouldn't let them struggle alone. Jesus met them in the storm and overpowered it. He even let Peter stomp on the waves with Him. When Peter's doubts caused him to sink, Jesus caught the disciple's hand and challenged him to trust His powerful care.

Being a Christian won't plop you into a calm sea tickled by a gentle breeze. It might stir up storms. And

Jesus' daring invitations sounds even crazier than rowing across a stormy lake or walking on water: *Know Me*, He says. *Live for Me.*

But Jesus *never* leaves you to face the winds alone. He's there when your faith means you sit alone because you can't stomach the nasty conversations in the lunchroom. He's next to you in the hallway at school when you find out a classmate killed himself or a girl you know well is pregnant. He's standing with you and your friends when you have to make gigantic choices. He's at your house when your family fights.

When darkness upsets your sense of direction, when winds scream and spray pokes your eyes, Jesus comes to you and says, "I'm not a ghost or a fantasy or too good to be true. I'm real. Don't be afraid! It's me! I'm here!" He cares for you, using His Holy Spirit, His Word, and other believers to lift you up.

Jesus is worth trusting. Not because He makes your sea smooth and your sky full of poofy marshmallow clouds—life doesn't always happen that way. He's worth your life because He's God's Son, who died and rose to stomp across waves with you, all because He loves you.

Do you want to keep growing closer to God? He feels closest when you're with Him on the waves, practicing prayer, courage, and action out in the winds, gaining a daring faith that transforms you into a worshiper and a wave-walker, not a weirdo.

Immediately Jesus reached out his hand and caught him. "You of little faith," he said, "why did you doubt?" And when they climbed into the boat, the wind died down. Then those who were in the boat worshiped him, saying, "Truly you are the Son of God."

MATTHEW 14:31–33

Acknowledgments

Thank you first to Lyn for loving me and ministering with me, to Nate for bringing toys to play with at my computer, and to Karin for hastening my writing. Lyn is responsible for more of this book than she will ever admit.

Thanks to our parents—Roy and Lois Johnson, and Tom and Pat Benson—and to our grandparents before them and our families with them—for the heritage of a faith that works . . . full of balance, grace, and love.

Thank you to Rev. Alvar Walfrid, Rev. Leland Evenson, Rev. Peter Yang and Rev. Jim Maines and their congregations for teaching me a pastor's heart.

Thanks to the professors and administration of the University of Wisconsin—River Falls, especially Dr. Larry and Jane Harred, and Lois Michaelson, and to the faculty of Fuller Theological Seminary, for stretching my thoughts and their expression.

Thanks to Jeff Johnson, Todd Wessman, Jim Papandrea, Dick Lee and Randy Horn and their families, fellow members of the Church of the Non-Bozos, for their sanity calls.

Thanks to the pastors and support staff at Elmbrook, especially Stuart Briscoe, Mel Lawrenz, and Dick Robinson, for believing in me and nurturing me, for making room for an abnormal Fuller graduate and for not yelling at me when I don't wear socks to church.

Thanks to Kit and Luann Marter, who quietly set the pace for Dave, Pete, and me in Junior High Ministry at Elmbrook Church.

Thank you to Charette Barta and everyone at BHP for working hard to make this a better book.

And thank you to Elmbrook's teachers, leaders, parents, and—most of all—the world's greatest students, for pressing on with me toward the goal of knowing God. May we take hold of Christ the way He's taken hold of us.

Kevin Walter Johnson